Building the Dream Team

Julia A. Royston

BK
ROYSTON
Publishing

BK Royston Publishing
P. O. Box 4321
Jeffersonville, IN 47131
502-802-5385
http://www.bkroystonpublishing.com
bkroystonpublishing@gmail.com

Published by: BK Royston Publishing LLC

ISBN-13: 978-0692310991

Printed in the United States of America

Dedication

I dedicate this to every person who has ever felt alone while striving to make your dream come true.

I pray that you receive the courage to keep going, strength from God to keep growing and knowledge from the masters to keep knowing.

Your dream team is on the way and I trust that God give you the wisdom and discernment to know the difference between a scream and your dream team.

Team

Same Goal.
Different Position.
Hard Work.
Teachable.
Driven.
Achievement.
Success.

Acknowledgement

I thank my Lord and Savior Jesus Christ for giving me another opportunity to introduce more people to you. I thank you that you have entrusted this gift to me. Lord, let your Spirit move through this book to the people who will read it.

To my husband, Brian K. Royston, the love of my life for loving and cheering me on so much that I can be and do all that God has placed in me. I love you...

To my Mom, who is a great support and to my Dad who is in heaven but, I know is proud of me and always encouraged me to go for it. Thanks to all of my family for their love and support.

A special thank you to Rev. and Mrs. Claude R. Royston for their love and support. Papa thank you for using your fine tooth comb to edit this book again.

This book is for every business owner striving to build a dream team for ministry, business, a non-profit organization or a family.

Love, Julia A. Royston

Table of Contents

Introduction

Build

The time, tenacity, talent, treasure, trouble and retrying it takes to get what your mind, heart and inner eye saw.

Julia Royston

The dictionary defines build as "to construct (especially something complex) by assembling and joining parts." Another definition is 'to found, institute, build, or bring into being on a firm or stable basis.' No matter which definition you choose it is not easy, it will take time and you should have a design or plan in mind to build anything. To build anything using objects, hardware or non-human materials is hard enough but, try building something with humans. They each have a personality. Each person has a preference, opinion, background, experience or preconceived notion on how to do anything. At times, each person wants to be or act like the leader. At other times, these same people get discouraged, don't want to participate or even do what it takes to get the job done. Building or assembling a team is not easy but, if you find a good team, fight with everything you have to keep that team together. The bible says that 'two are better than one and a three-fold cord can't easily be broken.' It will take skill, strategy and insight to make sure that you are getting the right people for the right position. There will be times even after you have made a decision you will doubt the decision to even ask or invite a person to join your team. How will they act? Will they get along with the others on the team? Will they along with me the leader? Will they hurt or help us? Will we get more or less accomplished having them on board? Can they really do all that they claim they do without tearing up what has already been assembled.

Building must be done piece by piece. It's not a race. Don't be in a hurry. If you find the right piece, great. If you don't find the right piece, person or product, wait on it. It would be better to build team right than to try to build wrong team fast. One of the first things that I always see in a building in a firm foundation. There are times that the foundation is laid and on the foundation can be seen for a long time. I have passed by buildings like this and wondered, 'when are they going to finish and put up the rest of the building?' Only the builder knows when the foundation is ready to have more built upon it. Establish a foundation, values, morals, rules, norms and regulations first for your team. Until all can buy in, follow, rehearse, team and train others about this foundation, you are not ready to build the walls, put in the wiring, windows or roof of your team.

The famous line from a movie, 'if you build it they will come' is a great saying but, knowing what to build is a whole other story. We all want to work with the best people, with the best skills that get the best results but, it will take building as much trust, confidence and camaraderie as possible to get the job done. As we begin to dig deeper into this book about building a dream team, begin by thinking about what you are trying to build? After the team is built, what do you want to accomplish with the team? How will you know when you have finished or accomplished your goal with the team?

DREAM

Big Dreams or a Day Dreamer?

Dreams happen to most people at night when they are sleep. Some dreams are very vivid and you can remember all of the details of the dream the next day. Some dreams are vague with some parts memorable and other parts of the dream you can't remember at all. There are some people that have their best dreams during the day. This dream is defined as 'an aspiration; goal; aim.' I call them day dreamers. These people can see with not only their physical eyes but, their inner eye. They see to invent, create, organize and strategize. The inner eyes are at times far clearer than the eyes located on our face. So as someone who will lead, be a part of or organize a team, what do you see? What is the goal or aim of your team? What should a member of your team aspire to do? If there is nothing to aspirate to, what will the individual team members being doing, working toward or striving to achieve? Furthermore, without knowing the goal, destination or purpose, how will you know when you have or have not obtained it? Be able to see a vision is one thing but, being able to understand clearly the vision the vision is something. What is the vision that you saw? How will you explain that vision that you saw to something else? Can the vision be drawn out with plans, a presentation or pamphlet? Does the vision have to be spiritualized and internalized before someone to receive it? Finally, after you know the vision and determine the vision that you saw, how will you convey that vision in such a way to others so that they can carry out the vision themselves, with or without you.

So again I ask, what do you see?

YOUR TEAM

Team

When it comes to the word 'team' several things come to mind. For me it is athletic sports. Sports is the mecca of teams. Whether it is football, basketball, baseball or soccer, it takes everybody working together, giving their best in their position to make the goal of winning possible. So if you are running an at home based business, an author of a new book, overseeing a ministry or a CEO of a major corporation, it will take a team of people, giving their best in their position to reach the goal successfully. The phrases "team work makes the dream work" or "there is no 'I' in team" are both very true. The bible even says that 'two are better than one and a three-fold cord is not easily broken.'

Many of us have heard these sayings for decades or longer but, the first thing to ask yourself is, do I work well with others? I have seen total introverts assemble a team and deep down they don't want to work with other people. How do I know? Because as soon as the team assembles and organizes itself, the person who assembled the team disbands the team. Team building takes self-sacrifice by putting the mission of the team first. Thus, as the leader, you will often put your personal needs and agenda on hold for the good of the entire organization. Are you willing to do that? Next, ask yourself another question, do you even like people? If you don't like people and try to work with people, you can become a user and manipulator which leads to control, misuse and abuse. Yes, you may need more hands to get a job done but, at what cost?

How do you get the right team to make that dream actually work? How do you get everyone on the same team instead of several 'I' focused people trying to get a job done? It takes practice, trial and error, risk taking and a strategic plan of what parts you need to have on your team to be successful. Furthermore, you must systematically and purposefully, looking for those people to meet your team's qualifications.

My goal with this book is to help you determine, discover and develop your dream team for your organization, product or service. The sky is the limit on how high, fast and far you wish to go, grow and expand.

Let's Start Building!

Team Means People

It may be quite obvious to some, but not as obvious to others, that a team starts with people. I am not going to assume anything when discussing this topic, so I am going to ask. Those of you who have a desire to build a dream team, do you even like people? I see people all of the time trying to work with other people and they don't like people themselves. I didn't say love all people. I'm just saying like some people.

My father predicted that he would die before my mother and he was a true prophet because he died in 2010. One thing he said often about my mother was that 'mama will be fine after I'm gone because she loves people.' My mother can hold a conversation with a stranger for a long time, whether they listen or are interested in her and the topic or not. Why? My mother is genuinely interested in people. She wants to know what they love, about their families, if they go to church, or even what they could possibly have in common. If you truly enjoy people, you will enjoy and strive to build meaningful relationships. If you don't enjoy people, you will be isolated and only build superficial, temporary and 'all about me and my pursuits' relationships.

Building, organizing and sustaining a team will involve a ground zero or starting from the beginning approach to team building. Team means people. You have to be ready, willing and able to deal with people. People bring with them good, bad, and often times, the situations around them to their work. Each particular situation and personality contributes to the person's ability to lead, make money, contribute or stay committed to a team. Are you ready to deal with all of the different personalities and nuances that people possess? With multiple people on your team, there will be multiple issues, personalities, preferences and nuances with which you must deal. If you say yes, you are ready to begin. If you say no, then I will be praying that you have the strength to perform all of the tasks of your business, organization or service yourself. Without a team, you will be creating, managing and performing the tasks yourself.

After all of the work you put in, I am quite sure that there will come a time when you realize it's time to start building your dream team.

You Need A Team

When I first began writing this book, I started out discussing the team purpose, goals, who's on the team, etcetera. I then realized that I needed to discuss the logic of putting together a team versus going it alone. Doing a task or project alone should be easier, right? You don't have to discuss anything with anyone. You just make a decision and do it. You don't have to worry about someone not doing his job because you are going to be doing everything. Think about it. Can you really do everything well? Some people will say, yes, of course. Be honest with yourself. No one does everything well. Building a team is more about gathering the 'people resources' that are necessary and qualified to complete a project, deliver a service or manage an event with excellence. Having a team around you does not say that you can't do things well. Having a good team around you that can do a job well says that you are a smart and wise person. It's not about you. You want what's best for the project, company, product or service.

So, when do you need a team? You will need a team from the very beginning of the product, project, company or service. Why? Because there will be some aspect of your business that needs a team perspective. For example, it is more productive if you have five people selling a product than just one. Therefore, even if you only need a team for sales or technology or information or advice, you still need to have a team in place with your business, organization or service. The size, expertise and skill set that will be needed from the team members will be determined by the infrastructure and needs of your business' products or services. If you handle all of the details and duties of your organization yourself, you will be tired and not necessarily productive. On the other hand, you should have some working knowledge of all of the activities required to make your business successful. Secondly, if you don't know all of the components it takes to run your business, when help comes, what will you tell them to do? Also, how will you know whether the work that they have done is effective or not? A team is necessary and should be utilized in some aspect of your business, organization or service, but your team should not know your business better than you do.

In the beginning of my publishing business, I did everything. I answered the calls, the layout of the books, the cover design, wrote the descriptions, contacted the printer, did distribution, marketing, promotions, performance, showcases, billing and sales. I did, literally, everything. After all of that work, I was tired mentally and physically. At the rate I was going, I would have been burned out before my first year in business. I realized that no matter how good I was at all I was doing, it was not a good use of my time. I had to determine what would be the best use of my time as the leader/CEO/visionary of the business. Next, what could someone else do for me that would economically continue and grow my company? As much as I loved the creative process, I couldn't do it all. I could approve, monitor and guide what was going on creatively, but I couldn't physically do everything that was required creatively. I also had to realize and surrender to the idea that there were other people out there with more and better ideas than I could produce on my own. Finally, I realized that if I were to obtain the services of others, I had to look at my fee structure. My clients would have to understand that I had to pay someone else on my team for a particular service. I couldn't absorb the costs as I did when I did the work alone. Therefore, my clientele suddenly changed with the new price structure. Additionally, the quality of the work changed with the addition of these new experts on my team. The completed works promoted themselves and the satisfied authors spread the word to others, which helped to bring in new clients to my publishing company.

Building a team of people to be a part of any facet of your business will make you critically and strategically look at yourself, your company's organizational structure, management styles, products and services. With the right team of people in the right place, your company can literally change overnight.

We will briefly take a look at the profile of a team member, you as the leader, how you work and what you really need around you to get the job done. Let's

go.

Reflection

Do You Need a Team?

_____

_____

_____

_____

_____

_____

_____

_____

_____

_____

_____

_____

_____

_____

_____

Team Member Profile

There is a difference between being with someone whose company you enjoy and people with whom you work well to get the job done. I have friends who are great shoppers and other friends who I wouldn't take on a shopping trip because they would cramp my style. However, I do have friends and family with whom I could travel the world because we have similar tastes, styles and interests. It is an enjoyable experience to be with these people on a casual, relaxing trip.

On the other hand, you do want to have a good business working relationship with those on your team, but it is not required to travel, shop or do other non-professional activities with these same people.

With that said, let's think about your business and who you are as a leader and personality type. Finally, think about what you are trying to accomplish and where you are going with your business. Now, think of who you need on your team who can do the job but can do the job with you. With putting these three questions together, your team make up may be totally different than your original thoughts about team members. You can meet, hire and bring on your team the most qualified, knowledgeable people in the world, but if your personality and work ethic can't properly utilize their skill set, you will get nothing done. Hiring a dream team for you and the dream team for someone else will and should be totally different teams. Who I can work with and who another business owner can work with requires two different types and characteristics in people.

With all that being said, now what type of people do you need around you to get the job done? What type of person will work best with you? Are you organized, detailed, oriented, schedule driven and methodical in your approach to business? Or, are you a creative person who works on inspiration, finds it hard to stick to a schedule and needs someone to handle the administrative and organizational tasks for you? These questions must be answered, and clear. A detailed vision for your team should be determined before you can even request the services of or begin the inquiry process for someone to join your team. Until you know who you are as an organization, business or service, how will you know who you are looking for, need and want on your team? With an unclear vision, mission and purpose, it will be very difficult for you to be prepared and ready to successfully operate a long-term, successful team.

The Team Leader

The leadership of any team is critical to the success of the team. If you are in a leadership role on any level, you need to evaluate yourself first as the leader. It doesn't matter whether you are leading a corporation, girl/boy scout troop or your children across the street, the success of that event will depend on you. The team will only be as effective as its leader. There are as many leadership styles as there are leaders. Everyone leads differently and brings their own personality to leading or being involved with people. I categorize my leadership style as Visionary/Team Leader/Co-Worker. This means that I can see and cast the vision for the project that I am leading. I meet with members of my team when necessary. I am quite accommodating of each team member and respect the team member's schedule and celebrate each of his abilities. I love to work with the most skilled, talented and able people I can find and afford. I am not intimidated if you are qualified. I love being around people who can think, create, plan and execute with excellence. I strive to provide my team with the tools, supplies, budget and plan to get the job done. I love to appreciate my team members in either monetary or gift form. Additionally, I am a team leader. That means that I am not going to ask you to do something that I either can't or won't do myself, if it is within my skill set. If it is a task within my skill set, I am a co-worker and I work alongside you in an effort to get it done.

What I am not is a dictator, egotistical, condescending and non-appreciative maniac. I don't like to work with or be around these types of people for any length of time. I enjoy people and strive to create an environment so other people can enjoy being with me.

I have told you a little bit about my leadership style. It is time for you to categorize your leadership style. With this study about teams, we are not trying to discover a new organizational industry term. We're just trying to describe, in general terms, your leadership style so you can easily explain it to your team.

Think about what type of leader you are? How do you lead? Do you lead as a dictator or by example?

Meaning, do you only tell others what to do and don't assist in getting the job done, or do you lead, work, contribute and chip in to help get it done? Do people readily want to work with you? Do people gravitate to you, your projects or plans quickly and easily by volunteering? Could you name ten people who you could call to come help you in an emergency? If you say no, then you need to look at yourself closer as a leader. There is a saying 'if no one is following you and you are the leader, then you are not a leader, but you're just taking a stroll in the park.' Some of you may say, yes, you can name ten people who would help you in an emergency, but you can't ensure that they would come because of the date, other obligations or prior commitments. It is true that people are busy and may not be available the time or the day you call, but the mere fact that you can call and they will answer your call to decline is good enough. If you don't know ten people to call, it means you have isolated yourself from relationships to make connections with people, and/or people just don't want to work with you. If the latter is true, that people don't want to work with you, stop building a team. Remember, as forestated, "Teams mean people."

How do you want to be perceived as a team leader?

Reflection

How do you want to be perceived as the leader? Furthermore, how are you perceived as the leader by others?

_____

_____

_____

_____

_____

_____

_____

_____

_____

_____

_____

_____

_____

_____

_____

Your Circle

We have determined that we need to know what type of people we work with as business owners. Now, we need to look at what types of people we attract? This is a hard question for some of you because you never have thought about or even looked at what types of people are in your life. You can't pick your family members, but you can pick your friends, business partners and associates. Think back to recess when you were in grade school. You were able to pick who you would play with or spend time with during recess. In fact, you may have been forced to participate in organized activities in gym classes in middle or high school. But, after school and lunch, you chose with whom you would eat and spend your free time. Think about the people in your life currently. What types of people do you attract and choose to spend time with now? Are the majority of the people you choose to spend time with outside of work financially broke, lazy, negative, and unethical in their business dealings or can't maintain employment? OR, are your chosen friends or associates financially secure, entrepreneurs, driven, ethical and positive? Your answers to these questions will define the team of friends you have already built and didn't realize it. If you don't associate with or come in contact with people who are business minded, upwardly mobile or striving to be successful in whatever their endeavor, you will find yourself just as unsuccessful. Now, I realize that every relationship or person you come in contact with shouldn't be solely for the purpose of moving your organization's agenda forward, but it can certainly help. Friends, as well as co-workers, can help move a business or career forward. Do not misjudge the part friends play in your life. Friends are indirectly a part of your team. Your friends represent and make a statement about you. Furthermore, you eventually take on the behaviors of the people you choose to be around. The old saying, 'birds of a feather flock together' is true. Based on the few pages you have read so far, you should be conducting a mental evaluation of the people in your life. Visualize the people with whom you associate, and if these people will in no way help you reach your business or organization goals, the next step is to start a search for a different circle of people. Eventually, you will attract people who have your same mind set, goals and aspirations. If the people already in your friends or associates circle are at their core, people who could help you, write down their names. Now, determine how they could possibly help you with your product, organization or ministry mission and vision. Remember the saying, 'many hands make light work.' The meaning of that is the more people you have promoting, giving good references and recommendations for a product, service or organization, the better. Before you start recruiting outsiders, start with the people who are already in your life and go from there.

The Law of Attraction

You have looked at the people whom you attract in your life. Have you ever asked yourself why you attract this certain personality of people in your life? Are there words that you say, actions you take or signals you are giving that draw certain people in your life? Furthermore, are these people drawn to you for your benefit or solely for you to benefit them? Finally, if you can't determine why you attract certain people on your own, ask someone who will be totally honest with you and you should have your answer. When I was younger, I had low self-esteem and I attracted predators who could detect a person who longed for attention and would take advantage. When my self-confidence and self-worth rose to a much higher level, it is amazing how the predator types suddenly disappeared. Now, I attract authors, young entrepreneurs/business people and worship leaders. Why? Because they are the type of people I meet at conferences, meetings, networking events which I attend and in which I am involved.

Sometimes we attract the wrong people because we are not in the right place ourselves to recognize the wrong people. In business, we may attract people who can't help us in our mission because the wrong people want what we have or see where we are going and want to tag along. There are others who just don't contribute to the mission but, oddly enough, want to gain the benefits of your company, product or service. These people are takers, groupies and unnecessary entourage. Be able to spot these people quickly. You will know them because they usually don't seem to have their own business, career, company or path. They are just following whatever you are doing. Additionally, they are experts on what you are doing, but their own mastery is limited.

At other times, we attract the right people and don't recognize them because we associate with the wrong people too long or because they came to us looking or acting differently than we expected them to act.

We attract the right people with contributing gifts, talents, abilities, but we are not in a position to utilize what these people have to offer because we are not ready emotionally, financially or organizationally. My hope is that you will look around you at the people you are already attracting. Ask yourself, what do they have to offer to support, uplift and further the mission and vision of your company, business, product or service? The second question is what are you missing that is not in your current circle of friends, family or influence? Pray that God will send those people to you to help further your mission and vision. More importantly, pray that you are ready to receive what they have to offer. There is nothing worse than getting the right or great thing at the wrong time. Why? Because you will either lose it, misuse it or abuse it. That last statement was worth whatever you paid for this book.

Reflection

_____

_____

_____

_____

_____

_____

_____

_____

_____

_____

_____

_____

_____

_____

_____

_____

_____

_____

Team Recruiting

Once you look at the people in your inner circle, it may be time to start recruiting new people for your team. If your team members quickly lose interest, show a lack of enthusiasm for the team's projects or just don't show up, it's time to recruit.

Do not bring anyone else onto the team without interviewing them first. It doesn't matter if it is your mother. Ask them why they want to be on your team and give them the requirements for being a part of your team. If you, as the leader, are not a good judge of character, bring in others who can better discern personalities. Interview each team member. All of the technology in the world cannot replace a good face to face meeting. I realize that you can't always be in the same place or room with the person, but SKYPE or FaceTime the person. There is something about looking into someone's eyes that helps you to get to know them better. You will never fully know someone until you work with them, but you do have some idea of chemistry or a sense of connection with that person.

Determine what you need each team member to do. What will be each person's role on the team? What do you want from your team? What should your team expect from you? What is the purpose of the team? What happens when one person is unable to function on your team? What happens if the leader is sick, incapacitated or dies while on your team? Will the team go on? What do you see?

What are the qualifications you are looking for and what is the skill set necessary to fulfill that role? Draft a job description for each team member. What resources do you think initially will be needed for each person? The needs of the team members will evolve and change because the needs of the team and the projects that are currently being worked on will change.

You might ask, what if I didn't get to select or choose the members of my team? What if, as some of the new NBA coaches this year, a team is already in place and you have to go with a team that is new to you but not new to the league? We will all find out what type of leader, coach, president or supervisor you are already. Let's go!

Reflection

_____
_____
_____
_____
_____
_____
_____
_____
_____
_____
_____
_____
_____
_____
_____
_____
_____
_____
_____

Team Diversity

Keep an open mind when selecting or recruiting your team members. Look for people with diverse backgrounds. Diversity brings different mindsets and totally different perspectives on various issues. A diverse team can prove very helpful in delivering your business or organization message to a wider audience. Having a diverse team, you will be able to communicate with, speak the language of, and understand the needs of people outside your comfort zone or immediate scope of influence.

In the United States, when people hear the word diversity, they immediately think diversity refers to ethnicity or race. An ethnically diverse team is wonderful and should be considered because of the global society in which we live. With technological advancements, we can communicate with people around the world in a matter of seconds. International connection can be productive and very profitable, depending on the team's purpose and mission. Additionally, team diversity should also refer to differences of thought, skills, gifting, talents, background, culture references and abilities, no matter the ethnic background. Team diversity is crucial to having a well-rounded and balanced perspective on issues ranging from problem solving, people management, time management and product creation. There can be team diversity even if all of the people on the team are of the same ethnicity. Be very strategic and intentional to find and embrace people different than the leader or core group of people. Initially, teams are formed with people who are alike, grew up alike or came from the same neighborhood. At the beginning of the team's existence, with so many commonalities, there will be a sense of comfort and trust. In the long run, the knowledge, exposure and ability to think outside the comfort zone will be very limiting. Eventually, the ideas will dry up and the fresh approaches to changes in the market place will cease because each of the team members has the same point of reference and ideas. A diverse team will bring fresh eyes, different approach and new ideas to the success of the team.

At times, you may lean toward selecting a person like yourself or one who would be typical or familiar in that position and lose out on the perfect person because his personality, dress or approach was different than yours. Stop and take the time to listen so you don't miss a jewel because it was not a cookie cutter of you.

As the team leader, you should strive to cultivate the skill of recruitment, development and retention of people who can bring results to your team. Additionally, the team members should be productive in mindset and bring a fresh approach to each task even if they don't align with your own personal agenda or match your social group of friends. The purpose of your team is to ultimately work together to get a job done and succeed rather than just finding people for social outlets.

Socializing is for time spent with your family, friends and other constituents and it doesn't always meet or fit in with your business needs.

Reflection

_____
_____
_____
_____
_____
_____
_____
_____
_____
_____
_____
_____
_____
_____
_____
_____
_____
_____
_____

A Team for A Task

We have already determined that you will need a team of some sort from day one of your organization or business. Also, look at the people you already attract to see if they have the makings of a good core team. Before we move forward, remember to look inwardly to make sure that you are ready to receive, cast vision and to develop the people to fulfill the mission of your business or organization.

In this chapter, we will discuss teams and how you need different teams or different levels of teams for different activities, roles and actions.

In sports, there are different teams established depending on the level of competition. There are intramural sports teams for people who are competitive and athletic but only want to compete on a certain level. On the collegiate level, there are Division 1, Division 2 and Division 3 schools that have specific qualifications and guidelines to adhere to in order to maintain their membership in each division. On the professional level, most sports have minor leagues or farm teams to prepare people for the next level of play or competition.

Next, let's take a brief look at the different levels or categories of people who can and should be associated with your company or business. I categorize these levels as the Inner Circle, the Outer Circle, the Competitive Circle and last, the Galaxy and Beyond.

The Inner Circle

The Inner Circle team is made up of people who, no matter what you are trying to do, will support you. You can be selling lemonade today, Avon tomorrow and Girl Scout cookies the next week. Whatever it is you are selling, trading, promoting or doing, they have your back. This may be family, friends or church family who truly believe in you. In spite of all of the emphasis on 'haters', there are still people in this world who will support you. I have the family to prove it. I have friends who support me as well.

Within this Inner Circle or Team, there should be an Inner, Inner circle that you can rely on, who will tell you the truth but are qualified to help you get the job done. Also, these people have bought into the vision, lock, stock and barrel. They genuinely care and want what's best for you and your vision. Some things they may say while telling the truth will stink but, after the initial shock, you will agree, it was the truth, and you will thank them. In the bible, Jesus had twelve disciples, but He also had three disciples, Peter, James and John, who were His Inner, Inner Circle. Those three were with Jesus on some very special occasions. Who is on your Inner Circle Team?

The Outer Circle

The Outer Circle Team members are also supporters, but they are extended family. They met you along the way of your journey. They believe in what you are trying to accomplish with your business, ministry or products. This group of people is supportive because they genuinely like what you are offering. They have tried your product, liked it and told other people about it. The Outer Circle are people who have a life of their own and may not be called on for every campaign, conference or event that you are sponsoring, but they will support you if they are available. These people are your fan base, your external team and those who will spread the word about your product or service to others.

Additionally, these same people may refer business your way because they like the way you handle your business, even if they don't buy the products or services themselves.

The Competitive Circle

I have found that in business, ministry or non-profit organizations, if you plan on being in business for a while, you will and should know your competitors. Your direct competitors have the same core customers you are trying to attract. Over time, you will be at an event with these competitors. They are doing what competitors do, compete. Make note of these competitors. Get their contact information. Be cordial to the people on staff. Get to know who the managers, CEOs, top sales staff are and the prices of their core products and services. This is your competitive circle. You ask, how can my competitive circle help me? First, this competitive circle keeps you on your toes and makes you work harder to stay ahead of your competition. Second, if these competitors have products or services that compliment your products or services, you should strike a deal to work together on a project or two. At other times, these same competitors should become strategic partners. Strategic partners are companies that have the same clientele but different products or services to sell to the same clientele. When you combine your efforts, create an event, share expenses that will attract more customers together than you ever could separately, then it is a win-win situation for all companies involved. Finally, there are some competitors who refer certain clients/customers to their competitors. Why? Because it is the satisfaction of the client that they are most concerned about and not the sale. For some smart and mature company owners, the completion of a project, delivery of a particular service or a desired product to their customers by a competitor is worth more than making an attempt to deliver an undesired product themselves. These people are held in my highest regard and respect because they realize their strengths, weaknesses and limitations. A prime example is when I worked in the Sears shoe department and a customer wanted a shoe that we didn't have in her size or color. I called JC Penney to see if they had the shoes this person needed. I knew if JC Penney had the shoes in stock, they would hold them for the customer to pick up. You might think this is crazy, but the next time that customer wanted shoes, she came back to me at Sears. Why? Because I met her need and helped her get the product she wanted and didn't try to sell her something she didn't want. The customer was assured that I would get her what she wanted whether I could sell it to her or not. Build a team and relationship with even your competitors so that the customer's needs will be met, and eventually, your need for profitability will be met as well through great customer service.

The Galaxy and Beyond

Team Purpose – Why does the team exist? Is the team's existence necessary? What are the goals of the team? Be able to clearly convey the purpose of the team. People buy into what they can understand and what they believe in. Have evidence, facts, information and reasoning to back up the purpose of the team. Do not be afraid to answer any questions about the team's purpose, even if the questions are controversial. In the society we live in, trust should be an important factor when conducting business. People should be skeptical of organizations they involve themselves or participate until the organization has proven itself. You should ask questions. In addition, you should ask for references. As a team leader or visionary, do not be frustrated by this, embrace it. As a team leader, you should want people on your team who are analyzers and think logically, who will scrutinize people and situations. It should begin with you. Finally, the team's purpose should be posted, promoted, documented and repeated every time the team meets. The team's purpose should be easily conveyed on every marketing outlet, promotional tool and on social media. The team's purpose should be clearly defined and associated with a logo, symbol or emblem, even if it is short-term.

Team Parameters

You should determine the limits, boundaries and guidelines of your team and the team members. Is your team a long term group or for a specific assignment or project? How will someone be removed from the team if his performance is unsatisfactory? What are the qualifications for people to be a member of your team? What are the various roles, departments or responsibilities that come with people who are a part of your team? What documents will you use to select, train and develop new team members? Setting limits, goals, boundaries and guidelines are good foundations for teams to thrive and succeed. There is nothing worse than people trying to get to a goal without any direction. Without parameters built into the team and people buying into the team, people will do whatever they want and whenever they feel like doing it. There will be total chaos on your team. Maybe your team does not need a six-inch binder of rules or regulations, but there should be some sort of structure in place to govern them. If a problem does arise, agreed upon procedures should be in place to solve the problem. How will the parameters be relayed to each team member? Is there a contract, agreement or packet of information to be received and signed that you agree to these stipulations when you join the team? Outlining the team's parameters, guidelines and boundaries will save each team member, from the leader on down, heartache and confusion.

Team Leader Parameters

As the leader of a team, there should be some set parameters as to your role, power, position, protocol and procedures when relating to the other team members. Everybody can't be the ultimate leader. My dad said, 'anything with more than one head is a freak.' There must be someone who is in charge and will have the final say, authority or power to approve. On the other hand, you don't want total incompetence around you and the only thinker on the team is you. Do you have an organizational structure that stipulates who has what decision-making power and when their power stops and someone should seek another person or position for a decision or information? Every team member should be able to lead in his particular area of expertise. Everyone on the team should have his own position and role that he plays within the whole scheme of the organization. We are all leaders but with different leadership skills and authority. I have been a part of teams that were not able to accomplish much because everyone wanted to be the leader, and therefore, the work of the team didn't get done. People will excel and rise to the occasion when given the authority, parameters and liberty to do so.

How do you want the team to access and interact with you as the leader? Do you have an open-door policy with your team, or do they have to make appointments to access you? Do all of the team members have your cell number, or just a few? A leader should have a good understanding of him/herself and their leadership style. The team leader's leadership style should be easily relayed and clearly understood by everyone on the team. The needs of a team will eventually change. Because of team member's needs changing, your role as the leader will change as well. In your time together, you should ask the team members what they need in a team leader. Your leadership role should be established and general but not set in stone. The needs of your team, the purpose, goals and strategies of the team will all play a part in molding and shaping you as the leader of a successful team. The leadership role of your team or any organization should be evolving and reevaluated often. Change is constant. As the leader, you should recognize change and embrace it. Use the changes to your team's advantage and not detriment. An immature leader wants everything to stay the same to their liking and benefit. A mature leader realizes that change should be anticipated. The key to the entire team's success will be to make informed and strategic decisions to implement these changes to preserve the team's purpose and very existence.

Tools to Get the Job Done

You have been very selective of who is on your team. More importantly, you have defined, explained, declared and relayed exactly what you need from each team and team member.

Now you need to determine what tools your team needs to get the job done. People with great qualifications can do nothing without the tools to get the job done.

Whether your team has a product to produce, an event to plan or a service to provide, the leadership of the team needs to provide the team members with the resources they need to succeed. If the leadership is unable to immediately supply those resources, the team needs to meet to determine how to raise the funds for those resources so they can succeed at their tasks. There is nothing worse than telling someone to do something, especially if they are volunteering, without the necessary resources to complete the task. There is the biblical story of the children of Israel given the task to make bricks without straw. (Exodus 5:7) Sometimes when you are a part of a team, organization or family, you feel like you are being asked to do things without the equipment or resources you need to get the job done. Team members will be more productive if the tasks they are assigned to complete have the tools necessary to get tasks done in a professional, proficient and timely manner.

Experienced and qualified team members should have experience using the tools, resources and supplies requested and thus, the training process should be minimal. Ask them what they need. Is there anyone on the team who will need some basic or extensive training, teaching or instruction before they get started using these tools? Have there been recent upgrades or modifications made to these same tools that need workshops or refresher courses held for team members? Determine what it will take to meet the team's needs. Are the needs of the team more human manpower, financial resources or better tools to get the job done? Don't assume that you know what it will take, find out. There may need to be adjustments made in your budget, organization structure and infrastructure to make these needs a reality. The industry that your organization is a part of may have made major changes that will dictate some new tools, resources, procedures and protocols to not only get the job done but to be competitive and be an industry leader. For example, the publishing industry has changed drastically with the changes in technology. Publishing houses that were accustomed to only hardbound or paperback books and magazines now have to contend with eBooks via Kindle, NOOK, Apps and other online delivery systems.

Technology has played an incredible role in change and needs in all industry areas. The rapid technology changes and demands for storage, speed and security have rapidly revolutionized how companies, organizations and services interact and deliver products to its clientele. The technology that is selected for the team should be a long-term investment and not resources wasted on 'here today and gone tomorrow' innovations. Be wise in your investments and even wiser with your capacity to grow, transform and transition when the need arises. Don't stay stagnant, stale and committed to how your team does things in the present because it to will change. Strive to stay in a constant state of preparation within your team's leadership, budget and infrastructure, to be ready to meet their fluctuating needs.

I don't mean to overwhelm you with all of this information, but you have to decide. Do you want your team to succeed or not?

Team Development

There is not a person anywhere who doesn't need improvement in some area of his life. Perfection is a luxury that only God can afford. Human beings should always be learning, growing and evolving. No matter what type of team it is and for what purpose, there is more to learn and a training program for it. Each organization, business or ministry, should offer an opportunity, and even encourage, the members to attend workshops, conferences or gain additional information. This additional information should be relayed to the entire team to help them all improve. There are always new techniques being developed that would help your team do their jobs better. They streamline procedures or even bring to your attention new legislative regulations for your business. The new regulations could possibly help grow the business.

In teaching, we call it professional development or PD for short. These workshops are usually three to six hours long. They are held during the summer and filled with new content and opportunities for practice as well as networking time to learn from other colleagues.

Summer development is best for teachers because this is the time that teachers can prepare for the upcoming school year and the needs of their students.

Each organization will have to determine what are the best training needs and time for each of their teams. For example, all teams need to be trained in some way, in some area, but all teams may not need to be trained at the same time. Some need training before or after a product release or prior to or after an event. No matter the content, need or purpose of the team, know that professional development is an essential and critical requirement for all teams.

Reflection

_____
_____
_____
_____
_____
_____
_____
_____
_____
_____
_____
_____
_____
_____
_____
_____
_____
_____

Be Flexible & Let the Team Go

Don't panic or hyperventilate when I say, 'let the team go.' I don't mean 'firing' the team or letting them run wild without any structure or guidance. Let the team go by letting them go to do, be and perform at their highest potential. There are some leaders who are intimidated by people with great abilities. They give a person an assignment that they could do and do well, but since they are afraid of the recognition, they take the assignment away from the abled person. It sounds crazy, but there are some ruthless leaders in the world on so many levels.

No matter what and how you categorize your role as the leader, you must allow the team members to do what they do best. Micromanaging a team is pointless. Why have team members who can't perform independently and immediately on your team? Yes, they may need coaching, guidance, redirection or more instruction, but at the core or foundation, they should be able to perform and fulfill their role. Why do you have them on the team? Are they there for show or for true progress? If you can't allow the team to perform or do what they do best, you may be the wrong leader for that team. A team's dynamic is that there are multiple people with input, skill sets, abilities and potential. As the leader of the team, you must allow them to complete their assignment even with the possibility of making a mistake. If there is an error, correct it. If you have selected the wrong person for a role or position, give that person a different assignment or just replace him with someone new. Be flexible enough to get the right people in the right positions doing the right things to get the right results. There is no way a basketball coach can effectively coach and play at the same time. The coach has to give instructions and suffer the consequences and successes of the team members' actions. Be flexible and let the team go!

Reflection

_____
_____
_____
_____
_____
_____
_____
_____
_____
_____
_____
_____
_____
_____
_____
_____
_____
_____
_____
_____

Celebrate Your Team

I don't know about you, but I love to celebrate. I am not much of a partier, but I go all out for birthdays, anniversaries and the holidays. Dressing up, going to a nice restaurant with good food and great company is my cup of tea. I love to be appreciated and love to appreciate others.

To build and keep your dream team together, make it a habit to celebrate the accomplishments and major moments in your team members' lives.

After a major project is completed, a milestone is reached or even individual goals are reached, there should be some type of celebration. It can range from chips and dip snacks to a full celebration dinner or to taking the whole team on a cruise for a week. Whatever the team leader or organization deems appropriate, it should be done. Why? Because team accomplishments should be celebrated. It is hard to keep a group of people focused on one goal, one vision, one dream and one accomplishment all at the same time. We have many examples of division in musical groups, companies and other organizations. We have seen thousands of lawsuits, divorces and years of worker strikes because of a disagreement on one issue or another.

Incredible things happen when we are all focused and driven toward the same goal and destination.

One Team Ends, Another Team Begins

No matter how close you follow the suggestions of this book on how to build a dream team, many teams will not stay together forever. Don't take it personally. It is just life. We hear of teams, companies or organizations that dissolve because of animosity, but some teams split for valid and understandable reasons. There were no arguments, fights or disagreements that led to the end of the team; it was just time. Some teams break up because the project, product or performance ended and the purpose for existence is no longer necessary.

Attend a cast party of a play that ended its run on the stage and you will know how it feels. There will be tears, laughter and recalling of mistakes or great nights on the stage, but in the end, the play is over and everyone goes home to something different and new. These same actors for the ending stage play will eventually find another play in which to act. They will join another team of actors to be a part of another team again. One stage play, team of actors or community ends, but another community, stage play or team of actors begins.

As the leader of team members, you have to understand that your team has the possibility of ending. The ending of your team in its current stage does not mean the end of your relationships with these people altogether but the end of your relationship with these people in the parameters of this team.

Have you ever noticed how rapidly businesses close and re-open their doors as another business or service? There are reasons why one business ended and another one opened. The hope is that the new business will be even more successful than the previous one. Why? Because you now have a wealth of experience, knowledge, mistakes, successes and failures from the previous business that you are bringing to the new business. Hopefully, you learned from all of those experiences and strive to not repeat these same mistakes. It is the same with creating or building the dream team. To build a dream team for you and your business, it will take all of the experiences, misunderstandings, miscommunication, mistakes, failures and successes to get it right.

Conclusion

Building the dream team is a process. The process takes time and can't be rushed. Building the dream team takes skill, prayer, instincts and experience. It is possible you won't get it right the first time. Some people you will ignore and they could be the very person who will take your organization to the next level. Some people you will gravitate to can lead your organization and team to disaster. Listen to that inner voice that says 'no'. Listen to that inner voice that says 'yes'. Listen to that inner voice that says 'leave them alone'.

Every person doesn't mean you good. Every person is not trying to destroy you, but you have to be careful when building your dream team. Take your time. Contemplate thoroughly. Decide slowly. Use wisdom. If you make a mistake, correct it quickly.

Your dream team is like a puzzle. The pieces of your puzzle are out there; you have the final picture in your mind and on paper, but make sure to match the right puzzle piece/person that fits best in the right place. It may take a long time to complete the puzzle, but getting it right will be worth it all in the end. Remember 'Team Means People.' Build Your Dream Team with the Right People and the Right People will Build You an Empire.

About the Author

Julia Royston spends her days doing what she loves, writing, publishing, speaking and coaching others to tell as well as monetize their message to the world. That is her Why.

"Helping You Get Your Message to the Masses and Turn Your Words into Wealth."

Her companies, BK Royston Publishing LLC, Julia Royston Enterprises, Royal Media and Publishing and Royston Book Fairs are the conduits that support all of her client's endeavors. To date, Julia has written 60 books, recorded 3 music CDs and Coached more than 200 to write and publish books as well as establish their own businesses.

She is the host of "Live Your Best Life" heard each Sunday morning at 10:00 a.m. EST on www.envision-radio.com and now syndicated on www.regiaradio.com at 3:00 p.m. WAT.

To connect with Julia via email, social media, her websites or to schedule a free consultation, visit solo.to/juliaaroyston.